THE STORY OF GREA

The Most complete of all late Medieval Manor Houses.

John Buckler's Watercolour view of Great Chalfield from North West, 1823

First published in the UK by Thumbnail Media
www.thumbnailmedia.com

ISBN: 978-0-9956982-6-0

A catalogue record of this book is available from the British Library

THE STORY OF GREAT CHALFIELD

Hugh Wright
2019

All proceeds from the sale of this booklet will be donated to the Friends of Great Chalfield

THE STORY OF GREAT CHALFIELD

Foreword

One of the joys of living in Great Chalfield is the enjoyment and happiness it provides to so many people. Hugh Wright's enthusiastic research reflects this enjoyment. This history of Great Chalfield provides most helpful and welcome support to the development and maintenance of our Arts and Crafts Garden.

Robert Floyd
May 2019

Aerial photograph (from a balloon) of Great Chalfield from the North

Introduction

The easy supply of water is the essential starting point for the story of this place. A leat, dug before the Norman Conquest, flows to its north to supply the upper moat or mill pond for a mill now gone. A stream, from which the leat was dug, forms its southern boundary. A well in the courtyard in the original centre of the house supplied its drinking water. An abundant spring rising in its grounds flowed into its fishponds. These all made it an easy place to live in.
Its origins are also to be found in the lives of three towering individuals. Lady Constance Percy (c1330-1419) inherited the first house on the site from a husband (she had four) who she drove to an early death by her unruly behaviour. The second was Lady Margaret Hungerford (c1408-1478) who as a widow lived to see both her son and grandson executed by the Yorkists in the Wars of the Roses. She was faithfully served throughout his long life by her almost exact contemporary Thomas Tropenell (c1408-1487), the third and by far the most influential figure in the manor's long history. He built for himself this fine manor house in the 1460s in time of war, taking full advantage of a place that was so easily defensible.
The story of the life of Thomas Tropenell and his reasons for building this house in his old age have been told elsewhere. This is an account of the lives and times of all the people who have lived in it after him and also of those owners of the manor who lived elsewhere but who, even so, contributed to its changing fortunes in peace and war in its first 550 years.

May 2019

Chapter One 1487- 1639

Thomas Tropenell, the builder of Great Chalfield, died in November 1487. In his will he left his property which was extensive to his twenty five year old son Christopher (c1463-1503) – apart from generous bequests to his patrons and friends. He also included 'one costly white bed with all its hangings to my daughter Mary'. His other two children, Humphrey and Anne, had died before he made his will and Mary had very likely been generously treated at the time of her wedding. Christopher was married to Anne Carew, herself a wealthy heiress from Nutfield in Surrey. We do not know how they were introduced, perhaps through legal contacts of his father's in Lincoln's Inn where both Christopher and his father were members, Thomas was admitted 1470, Christopher in 1482. The life of Anne Carew has been extensively researched. Their lives set the scene from the end of the Wars of the Roses when this story begins. Both Anne and her husband's wills survive and we can learn much from them.

A surprising amount of Christopher's consists of detailed instructions for his funeral service in St Bartholemew's Corsham with variations depending on which day of the week he dies. This is an interesting window onto late medieval Roman Catholicism. The last item in it is unusual. He left his armour, singly itemised, to Lord Walter Hungerford. The Hungerfords employed his father from his youth and he died in their service. Christopher was made a Knight before 1500 – as is made clear in documents relating to his property in Nutfield, brought to him when he married Anne. These, with the Wiltshire property he inherited from his father, made Christopher a considerable landowner. Hence his Knighthood and his possessing a

Knight's armour. There was a property qualification for Knighthood which carried with it certain financial and military obligations. His father, wishing to avoid these, had turned down this privilege twice to avoid them and had been 'dis-trained' or fined for doing so. He believed in keeping a low profile politically in dangerous times. Two previous Lord Hungerfords, his employers, were brutally executed by the Yorkists in the Wars of the Roses so you can see why. The sixteen years that Christopher owned the manor, 1487-1503, were set in the domestic peace established by the Tudors. Armour for men like Christopher, a Knight, was losing its practical purpose. But it was still clearly required - more so for the likes of Walter Lord Hungerford, who might use it, at least for jousting. This was perhaps the reason for Christopher's bequest to him. Christopher was buried in St Bartholemew's, Corsham where his father and mother were also laid to rest in a fine tomb. The carving on the chancel screen there and its porch bear a strong resemblance to the porch of the manor and the carving under the oriel of the family bedroom at Great Chalfield and it is not too much to assume that they were also a gift from this generous family.

Anne Carew's will is much longer and gives much more detailed information about the family and her property in general. She was wealthy and clearly a good manager. Their wills tell us a lot about their characters. When Christopher died in 1503 their son, another Thomas Tropenell, was a minor so Anne administered the estate for him. She did a very good job, judging by the number of sheep, cattle and gifts she left to those she wished to remember. She left her son a rich man, like his grandfather. Her bequests included enough to educate at Oxford 'fyve bachelor scolers of divinitye' for twenty years and a new bridge at Staverton! It probably is still there. She also left to her daughter Elizabeth Hall a lot of bedding and carpets. One of Elizabeth's descendants, John Hall of Bradford on Avon, was to buy the manor and keep it in the family one hundred years later.

The next person of note in the story of the Manor is also a woman, Anne Eyre nee Tropenell, Christopher's granddaughter. She inherited the Manor from her father in 1553 in very unusual circumstances. We learn how this happened from a note inserted many years later into the Cartulary (Thomas Tropenell's portfolio of title deeds and legal documents that returned to the Great Hall in 1923). Someone must have found it strange. Her brother Giles, who was the heir to the manor, hung himself while out hunting. The note reads, "Putting one end of a pair of dog couples over his head, running after his sport and leaping over a hedge, the end of the dog couple that hung at his back took hold to a bough and kept him from touching the ground until he was strangled". Giles's mother was alive at the time and there is no record of her complaining about how it happened so it probably was just an accident – he was only just over twenty.

Anne Eyre and her husband John added panelling to the dining room and so covered the remarkable two dimensional wall painting of Thomas Tropenell.

The Initials of John & Anne Eyre on their dining room ceiling

The plaster ceiling still bears their initials. They also put in a bigger fireplace in the Solar – no doubt there was an element of competition with their neighbours the Long family of South Wraxall, who had just done the same in a far more elaborate way. John Jewel, Bishop of Salisbury (1522-1571), appointed Bishop in 1560 early in Queen Elizabeth's reign when he had returned from exile on the continent, described John Eyre in 1564 as 'no hinderer of the true religion'. That makes John a Roman Catholic who did not cause offence and went along publicly with the prevailing Protestant tide. So did his son and grandson. John Jewel had been appointed to suppress the externals of Catholicism but even so exceptions continued to be made for those like the Eyres whose public services showed they were loyal to the crown. The parish church register of All Saints Great Chalfield for this period survives. It is in parchment, as ordered in 1597. Entries from before then must have been copied out of an earlier paper register.

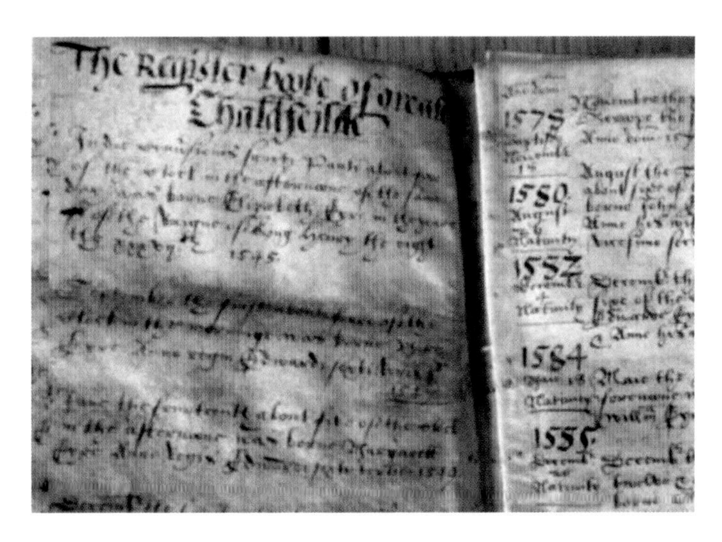

The first entries in the All Saints Great Chalfield Register, transcribed onto parchment 1597. The records in it from 1546-97 are only of the Roman Catholic Eyre family

It is in the Wiltshire and Swindon History Centre in Chippenham. Such registers were begun in 1538 in Henry VIII's reign when Thomas Cromwell ordered each Parish to keep records of marriages, baptisms and burials. The order was repeated in 1547, just before the Eyres became owners of Great Chalfield.

The Earl & Countess of Somerset, Howard relations of Anne Eyre

This register was mainly to show that Parish Priests were practising infant not adult baptism. It became in John Eyre's time not a record of all baptisms, marriages and deaths in the Parish, which it should have been, but only a record of the dates and times of day of the births of the Eyre family children.

The other local families in the parish were perhaps keeping clear of this Roman Catholic stronghold. It was used normally after 1603 when James l came to the throne. By then William Eyre, John's eldest son, had taken over on his father's death. The next link of the house to Thomas Cromwell came in 2015 when it was used as his town house, Austin Friars, in the BBC adaptation for TV of Hilary Mantel's *Wolf Hall*.

Sir William Eyre's tomb in All Saints Great Chalfield 1629.
The lettering on it has decayed

Sir William, as he became, who was listed in 1598 as one of the most important gentlemen of Wiltshire, married the aristocratic Lady Anne Baynton, a member of the Howard family whose seat as Dukes of Norfolk was Arundel castle, as it still is. They remain the leading Roman Catholic family in the country. Sir William inherited the house in 1581 and built on the very solid foundations laid by his father John, who had been High Sheriff and an MP. William owned the house for 48 years and lived in it with his large family, born from two of his three marriages, longer than anyone else has done. This was the high point in the fortunes of the house until modern times. It is surprising that no traces of a fine garden in the Tudor style survive. Recent ground surveys have not shown underlying structures other than plain walls. Sir William, as he became, was like his father an MP and was also the High Sheriff.

He died on August 24th 1629 and is buried at All Saints, Great Chalfield. He deserves to sleep well, unlike his eldest son, Sir John, who had mortgaged it by 1630 on the expectation of inheriting it from his father, to raise funds. He was always short of money. An attempt by Sir William before he died to avoid its going out of the family by disinheriting him must have alarmed John's creditors. They doubtless helped him to overturn this second will in the London courts, where they had influence, so he got Great Chalfield back, subject to his step-mother's life interest.

Sir John's extraordinary life (1580-1639), as a courtier and ambassador in Constantinople, has been fully researched by History of Parliament. Much new information has come to light. His life was divided into three unequal parts and was mostly spent in London or abroad. Through his mother he was extremely well connected. The Howards were just coming into royal favour at the Stuart court so he arrived in London, after his mother's death, in 1599, just at the right time. That and very likely his good looks were going strongly for him. All the favourites of James 1 were good looking.

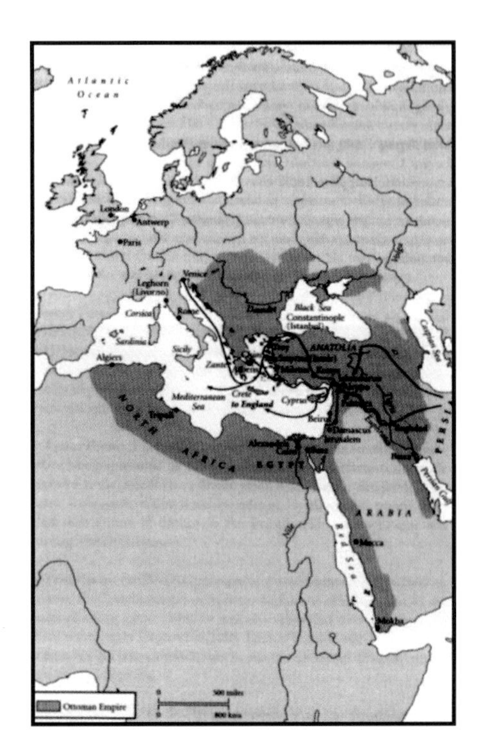

Constantinople (Istanbul) the capital of the Ottoman Empire, the trade route to England in the 17th Century & a dervish

His wife was a Lady in Waiting to the Queen. She was a member of the very distinguished Bulstrode family so she was well connected too – they married without her parents' consent. His father acquired a house in London through his second marriage so they may have lived at least for a time in that. John was Knighted aged 25 in 1605 at the very beginning of the King's reign just before going on an embassy to Spain with his uncle Charles Howard. He was elected as MP for Cricklade in 1614 though Parliament seldom met in those days and he only spoke once, recommending at the end of the debate on it an increase in the King's allowance.

It was doubtless his experience in Spain that led in 1619 to his appointment as Ambassador to Constantinople aged 39. This appointment lasted only two years and was his last though he remained a favourite at court. The importance of this post and Sir John's rapid fall from grace while there need explanation. The importance of Constantinople in our national affairs began in the reign of the previous monarch, Elizabeth 1. Her relations with the Catholic powers of France and Spain were complicated after her father Henry Vlll broke from the Roman Catholic Church and control by the Pope. She therefore felt free to open trade links with the 'infidel' Ottoman Turks whose capital was then called Constantinople, where Roman Catholics were forbidden by the Pope to trade. The contact developed rapidly. A 'Levant Company' was formed in 1592 by a merger of the Barbary and Venice companies. This was refounded by James 1 soon after his accession. This held the monopoly of trade from London to the Ottoman Empire. Under Elizabeth by 1600 it had twenty ships annually exporting cloth worth £150000 to the Mediterranean. It was mainly shipped to the rapidly growing centre of this trade, Constantinople, which had a bigger population then than any other capital in Europe. Sir John went there in the next reign as a relatively young ambassador.

By the time Sir John was there these trade links were developing rapidly. They were to become the most valuable that we had in the second half of the century only declining with the loss of power of The Sultan in the next century. But for nearly a hundred years we supplied the vast majority of the cloth the Ottomans needed, much of it for their rapidly growing army. They supplied to London spices, raisins (in very large quantities) and above all silk from their suppliers in what is now Iran and Iraq. After the restoration of the monarchy at the end of Cromwell's Puritan Commonwealth silk became the fashion and they were the sole suppliers of it before the trade along the Silk Road from China developed other outlets.

Trade with the Ottoman Empire was called The Turkey Trade. The appointed agents and merchants of the Levant Company in the ports there and especially in Constantinople often became rich.

Levant company agents

In witnesse

John Eyre

Sir John Eyre's signature on the Indenture mortgaging his father's manor.

They married local wives and adopted local dress – they were nicknamed Pashas as a result. Huge fleets of cargo vessels were sent as time went on twice a year from London escorted by our navy which increasingly and crucially controlled the sea routes to the Near East.

We owed that to Elizabeth's foresight and Samuel Pepys' naval reforms.

The Levant Company liked to nominate the ambassador and they were responsible for paying him. Unfortunately for Sir John Eyre, James 1 decided to nominate him without consulting them. What is more he told him to go to the Topkapi Palace soon after his arrival and tell the Sultan that he should desist from recruiting an army to invade Poland.

King James I was exceeding his authority in both cases and Sir John suffered as a result. He was heavily blamed by both sides of the disputes that followed. He was not paid, had to seize company goods to get any money for his embassy and fell foul of the Sultan as well, which was very dangerous. He was recalled in 1621, much to his relief, after two tumultuous years. He was cleared of all charges on his return but his finances, always on the weak side, instead of being enhanced by this move, which he had had good reason to expect, never recovered.

His successor Sir Thomas Roe was a gifted professional diplomat who became rich and famous. Sir Thomas's reputation, gained from previous success with the Mughal emperor at Ajmer in India, was just what was needed to settle things down. The sad thing is that it is clear from letters Sir John wrote while in post to colleagues, in particular to Sir Walter Aston who was then Ambassador in Spain, that he was competent and well able to do the job if he had had a level platform to start with.

On his return Sir John needed financial support. The King did what he could with minor gifts, such as control of Valentia Island off the south west shore of Ireland which enabled Sir John to import and export without paying tax on Valentia Island, though there is no record of his name either there or in the archives in Dublin. Where have we heard of that sort of thing before? He does not seem to have taken advantage of this. Later he was given a licence by the king to travel abroad – useful for promoting contacts for trade. But he was always short of money. We do not know exactly why. Rich and powerful friends were needed. Sir Richard Gurney, a future Lord Mayor of London, was one. Some time before 1630 he lent Sir John £3700, with Great Chalfield as security. The signed indenture forming security for this loan survives and is in the Wiltshire and Swindon History Centre.

The Royal Exchange , London in the 17th century. Laine Marly © The Museum of London

Sir John inherited in 1629 the manor from his father and used it as security more or less straight away. His involvement with the Turkey Trade doubtless brought him and Sir Richard together – Sir Richard was a mercer, the professional name for merchants who dealt in cloth, and he had a Silk Mercer as his Master. So Sir John's time in Constantinople did help him eventually. His mixing with such men in the Royal Exchange in the City was how business of all kinds was done. Sir John Eyre never really recovered from his time in Constantinople. But using these contacts and his friendship with the King he retained his post in the Privy Chamber, became MP for Calne

in 1625/6 and again for Chippenham in 1627/8. He gained his license for foreign travel in 1632. We do not know for certain if he used it and if so where he went.
We learn from the indenture of the loan from Sir Richard Gurney of 1630 two important things about the occupants of the house at this time. There was a sitting tenant 'for divers years', Sir Humphrey Forster with his wife and sixteen children. The Forsters' house, Aldermaston Hall, was being rebuilt. He was a relative of Sir John's wife and she was doubtless doing him a favour. Sir John's step mother, Anne, who had dower rights from his father's will, was also living there. Under these rights she could stay there for the rest of her life. The East and south wings, demolished during or after the civil war which was to follow, were still in use then but even so the house must have been full - as it had been for many years when Sir William lived there with his family of ten children.

Another relative of Sir John's wife, Sir James Whitelocke, is recorded as describing Sir John as '*one of the most dissolute, unjust and vicious reprobates that lived on the face of the earth'*. This opinion may have been formed over this tenancy in a mortgaged property, though he gave other grounds for deserving it. In his will he left only £250 in cash of which five shillings was to go to his wife! Aldermaston Hall was rebuilt between 1618 and 1636. We do not know when the Forsters first arrived at Great Chalfield, presumably soon after Sir William died in 1629. They were there by 1630 and presumably left to return to their own place when it was completed in 1636. They were the Manor's most distinguished tenants. Sir John Eyre died aged 59 in 1639, three years before the beginning of the civil war. He never lived in the house after he left it aged seventeen and he never repaid the mortgage on it, so it became the property of Sir Richard Gurney on Sir John's death. His stepmother will have continued her life there after 1629. She saw it through the Civil War (payments to her are mentioned in the garrison's accounts when they were stationed there during the Civil War) but we lose sight of her after the war until her death in 1654.

Anne Eyre's tomb. All Saints Great Chalfield 1654.
The Lettering on it has decayed

The executors of Sir Richard Gurney sold the Manor in 1649 to recover the loan, which may well have been when she moved out.

With this sale, as the dust of the Civil War was settling, the chapter in the history of the Manor begun at the death of its builder in 1487 can be said to come to an end. Those who bought it later might be related to him but they did not live in it like the six generations of Tropenells and Eyres had done. The ownership by Sir Richard Gurney was a brief interlude. The first chapter really came to an end when he acquired it in 1639 on Sir John Eyre's death.

Chapter 2 1639 – 1769

After Sir John Eyre died Civil war became increasingly inevitable in the years that followed. The local landowners divided themselves between the two sides in this war when it came. The Hungerfords and the Bayntons of Bromham were for Parliament. They switched to the side they thought would win, in 1642 just before the fighting started. Sir Edward Baynton and Sir Edward Hungerford both became Parliamentarian commanders. The Eyres, who remained in the area though not in Great Chalfield, and the Longs of South Wraxall were for the King. Sir Richard Gurney, now the absentee owner of Great Chalfield became Lord Mayor of London in 1641. It was hoped he could swing the City Bands behind the King, though the capital was generally for Parliament. He failed in this despite spending a fortune on the project and his Manor of Great Chalfield became a significant prize for the Parliamentarians. Sir Richard died in 1647 in the Tower during the war. This was three years after his Wiltshire manor had been selected by the Parliamentarian Major General of the West, Edward Massey, as a Garrison for 260 men with their 120 horses. They occupied it for two years from August 1644. to September 1646, though there was a brief time when a Royalist troop moved in with little damage to the property from either side. This was very fortunate. Other houses fared much less well.

We know of five other garrisons in the area, all Royalist. The appeal of the use of garrisons to their commanders was partly financial. Those in them were on half pay. Away from them fighting was often fierce. The Royalists subjected Salisbury to three days of terror in December 1644 when every type of

Edward Massey

vandalism and atrocity occurred. The Bayntons' great house near Bromham was destroyed and so was Pinnel House near Calne and Rowden Manor, a Hungerford House in Chippenham. Great Chalfield was more fortunate. It was occupied for a few days by the Royalists who then voluntarily withdrew and later endured a very short siege with few shots fired. In general, with its original security and moats so cleverly designed by Thomas Tropenell, the garrison there was left unmolested.

It is not hard to imagine the feelings of Anne Eyre who must have been there throughout. The financial accounts of the garrison, which survive in full in a contemporary fair copy, show that she achieved good relations with them. She was politically on neither side which helped and she agreed terms for the pasturing of their horses. The garrison was clearly a well ordered and disciplined community. They made repairs to the bridge over the moat and even paid the locals to help with the earthworks they made, presumably to the East and West where it was undefended by water. There is no record of any changes they may have made to the house itself. Perhaps it was then that the South and East wings were removed to assist with sight lines, perhaps it was after the war when its present L shape became common. A similar change was made at Westwood Manor just after the war by the Hortons, a wealthy family of cloth makers, who owned it then. A member of the Horton family was to be the first tenant of Great Chalfield after the war. Perhaps he made the suggestion to its new owner. The original ground plan of the service wings that were removed can still be seen in the pattern of low walls south and east of the courtyard well. Low walls also mark the foundations of the early medieval dovecote that was also removed at this time. It was replaced by a new one after the war, above the ancient

The accounts of the Great Chalfield Garrison

gatehouse. Had the soldiers in the garrison eaten all the pigeons and their eggs so they had to start again? An intriguing thought.

The best evidence for how the house was treated during the war is from what happened after it. Sir Richard Gurney's executors claimed damages before they recovered the mortgage on it. Thomas Hanham paid off the mortgage to the executors of Sir Richard Gurney for £3900 in 1649 after the execution of Charles ended the Civil war in England.
It will have needed refurbishment after being used as a garrison, so the Hanhams were ideal owners. They were and still are a prominent family in Dorset connected locally through marriage. Thomas Hanham's sister had married Sir John Horton of Broughton Gifford and so had become a neighbour of the Eyres. They were knowledgeable about property and well disposed. Is it possible to detect the hand of Anne Eyre, by then a very established lady in the county, in finding someone so suitable to buy it? She had lived in it ever since she married Sir William Eyre in 1626 so she must have been by then extremely well known and probably very persuasive. She quite literally 'knew where all the bodies were buried'. It is very likely that she also played a part in attracting distinguished local tenants to move in after the war.

Since this is such a key moment in the history of the house it is worth pausing a moment in the year 1649 and becoming a fly on the wall to watch an imaginary gathering that might easily have taken place at Great Chalfield in the spring of that year. Those present would consist of a party from Dorset who may have stayed the night before in a Horton relative's manor house at Broughton Gifford, then quite new as it had been built by their host there in 1627-1629. In order of seniority (doubtless they met for a meal seated in that way at table in the Great Hall) they could have been: Thomas Hanham the elder (1576-1652), a retired naval explorer of the East Coast of America whose home was in Wimborne Minster and his son, Thomas Hanham the younger (1617-1650), a London Lawyer then aged thirty two. The family were trying to recover their property in Dorset after it had been sequestered as a penalty for their loyalty to King Charles, especially when he was in Oxford, a Royalist stronghold. Thomas the elder. who was MP for Minehead, had attended the Oxford parliament. This was the 'crime' for which he was subsequently imprisoned and fined. That loyalty to the King would have appealed to the Eyres and to the late Sir Richard Gurney, whose executors had a strong interest in the result of this meeting. All there were Royalists and it was only three months after the execution of Charles 1.

The younger Thomas was the main man on this occasion. He had the experience, shared with those who owned Great Chalfield, of the Parliamentarians taking over his property. It could possibly have been put to him by his hosts that he should pay off the debt, secured on Great Chalfield, of the late Sir John Eyre to the executors of Sir Richard Gurney. Its treatment during the war would have excited his sympathy and interest in it as a fellow sufferer of such treatment.

Both Thomas Hanham the younger and his father as we now know, were to die in the next three years - Thomas the younger very sadly before his father in 1650, aged thirty three after only four years of a childless marriage to Margaret Dodington. His widow was to marry Edward Horton, her first husband's cousin and the first tenant of the manor house after the end of the war. Hers is also a sad story. Her father, Sir William Dodington of

Braemore House near Southampton, became obsessed with guilt, believing that a succession of tragedies in the Dodington family over two generations were the result of their house's being built on the site of a monastery destroyed at the Dissolution of them in Henry VIII's reign. In expiation he spent all his money on the Church and good works. Both Edward and Margaret, who were then related by marriage can be imagined as guests at this important meeting. They were to live in Great Chalfield as man and wife for the rest of their lives.

The hostess in the Great Hall would have been Anne Eyre. She had been living there for more than twenty years, most of them as a widow and would have described what it was like to be there with the garrison in the recent war. She would also have been anxious to commend the house to the visitors by speaking of its great days when her late husband owned it. She also doubtless would have suggested ways of making it good to live in again. Jane Horton, who was a Hanham, would have been there. Her husband had just built the manor at Broughton Gifford and would have brought her uncle and cousin over from there to meet her neighbour just a few miles down the road. She would have been very keen for her cousin from Wimborne to acquire the house – he might even leave it to her son! Her husband Sir John Horton would have been there. Despite being related to the Parliamentary general of the same name he had not played any part in the war at all and so had lost no property in it. He would have been good on finance and had built his own manor house twenty years before. Edward, his second son, had inherited a childless uncle's money and would have been an important guest. He hoped to move in soon as a tenant. He could have talked to his cousin Thomas Hanham the younger about changes that could be made before

The new dovecote now a gatehouse, mid 17th century

or after he moved in. Doubtless Sir John Horton would have suggested who paid for what. They may have toasted the King – if that was not too dangerous a thing to do in the year after his execution. More safely they could all discuss the placing of a new dovecote to replace the old one - the one built after the war even has echoes of the Hortons' Broughton Gifford manor - the changes that needed to be made to the south front and the removal of the earthworks put up to the east and west of the site by the garrison in the war. They may well have expressed annoyance that one of the bells of All Saints church was missing, perhaps melted down by the garrison. The one remaining was cast by RP Purdue of Bristol in 1622. They could also have discussed farming and past links with the house of their families. Above all the Dorset party needed to be tied into the project that had been put to them earlier of paying off Sir John Eyre's embarrassing debt (his step mother was keen on that, to restore the family name) and of putting the house to rights after the war. Underlying all the conversation the Wiltshire party would have been anxious to commend local society to these relatives from Dorset.

They all got what they wanted. Thomas Hanham the younger became the next owner, the debt was paid off and Edward Horton became the next tenant, just down the road from his mother. Perhaps to her disappointment he did not inherit the house when his cousin, Thomas, died so sadly in the year after he acquired it. It went to another cousin who lived nearer and was under ten years old, Sir William Hanham, as he became, of Dean's Court Wimborne. Edward Horton duly leased the manor from his young relative. Edward was a man of substance and probably had a big hand in refurbishing the house after the war as his cousin was only a boy at that time. Edward

Margaret Horton’s tomb in the side chapel of All Saints

Horton became High Sheriff of the county in 1660. His wife Margaret nee Dodington, died in November 1670 aged about 40. She was buried in the side chapel floor of All Saints Great Chalfield.

Sir William Hanham, the owner, died in 1671, the year after Edward Horton moved out to spend his last few years in Broughton Gifford. William Hanham instructed his executors to sell it, so the debts he had secured on it could be paid off and his wife could be provided for. After this sale just as had happened in 1649 when his uncle Thomas Hanham bought it to pay off a debt secured on it, another highly suitable and wealthy relative came forward to do the same. In this case he was a direct descendant of Thomas Tropenell, John Hall of Bradford on Avon.

Both the Horton and the Hall families were well established in Bradford on Avon and owed their wealth and prominence to the manufacture and sale of cloth, the main local industry for hundreds of years. Such people were called clothiers and some became very wealthy indeed. The valuation of John Hall's estate made in 1710 for probate survives in the British Library and shows the extent of his wealth. It was valued at £62369, about half in manors and houses of note, about half in smaller properties in and around Bradford on Avon and round the Abbey in Bath. These were rented out to those who made the cloth, which was a cottage industry on a grand scale. The mills on the river Avon which he also owned were for fulling, thickening, the finished product by machines driven by water-power. Great Chalfield was a major acquisition but only one of many.

The secret of this prosperity can be traced to developments in the way cloth began to be made in the west of Wiltshire and the east of Somerset in the 1580s in a small way and grew rapidly as the next century progressed. Demand for this new type of cloth caught on because of its quality. It attracted the attention of the Ottoman Sultans in time so the Turkey Trade of our cloth for their silk and currants grew on the back of it. Another important cause for this change was that farmers here were switching from pasturing sheep for their wool to growing cereals to feed a growing population. English wool became scarcer so demand for foreign wool grew. Spanish wool in particular was finer and cloth made from it was lighter and warmer. They had been using it on the continent for a long time and dying it in attractive colours. A few local cloth makers, notably John Ashe of Freshford, saw a commercial opportunity. Expert Huguenot craftsmen from the continent were brought in to show local workers how to make the new cloth.

The Hall, Bradford on Avon, John Hall's family home.

Fine Spanish merino wool in ever increasing quantities was imported into west country ports, the nearest to Spain, and brought from them to a growing number of places in the Avon Valley. Paul Methuen, described by the Wiltshire antiquarian John Aubrey when he died in 1667 as the greatest clothier of his time, married John Ashe's daughter Grace and brought the manufacture of it to Bradford on Avon in the 1650s.

The Hortons and the Halls were not far behind. Rolls of the new cloth, dyed for the most part red, were called salisburys. They were almost all exported from London by the Levant Company which sent two merchant fleets a year to Ottoman ports. From 1661-71 an average of 13672 cloths were sent each year. By 1672-7 this figure had climbed to 20075 per annum. This paid in part for the 280000 pounds of silk coming annually in the other direction. Domestic demand grew too throughout the century, especially when the imported silk became fashionable after the Restoration of the monarchy by Charles II. He promoted both the new cloth and the silk from the Levant by wearing them himself. This continuously growing domestic demand offset loss of sales of the cloth made from Spanish wool when the power of the Ottoman sultans began to erode towards the end of the century. The Ottomans lost control of the silk route through Persia. This eventually spelt the end of the Turkey Trade. Already in the 1740s the clothiers of Bradford on Avon and Trowbridge were complaining to parliament about the decline in their Levant trade. Nothing could be done about it and by the early years of the 19th century the great days of the Levant Company were only a memory. At its zenith it was the most valuable British trade of all and it helped to make the local cloth industry very valuable too.

Sir Paul Methuen c 1672 - 1757 in silk imported from Turkey, he moved from Bradford on Avon to Corsham Court in 1745

The Hall family was better placed than most to profit from this expansion of demand for their cloth. They owned the mills on the river just below their great house, called simply The Hall, in the centre of Bradford on Avon. John became so successful that he married into the local aristocracy. His bride was brought up in Longleat. She was a daughter of Thomas Thynne, the Marquess of Bath and one of the richest men in the country. John Hall became High Sheriff of the county in 1670. The Hortons were not far behind. Sir John Horton, (1593-1667), one of the wealthiest and most acquisitive of this very acquisitive clothier family, built for himself the fine manor house in Broughton Gifford. Edward Horton, the tenant of Great Chalfield until shortly before John Hall bought it, was his second son. The Hortons also made great changes to Westwood Manor just up the road from Iford Manor another of their houses. When Sir John Horton was High Sheriff in 1617 he described himself as of Iford, Westwood and Chalfield. Edward Horton when High Sheriff in 1660 described himself as of Great Chalfield. These families were leading the area into unprecedented prosperity, the Methuens most of all. They moved into Corsham Court and became very grand.

They supplied in the next generation influential ambassadors to Portugal and Spain who were more successful at this than Sir John Eyre had been as Ambassador in Constantinople at the beginning of this era! Spanish wool was behind all this. It was exported mostly from Bilbao and exempted from import duty from 1652. All the clothiers using it enjoyed the advantage this gave.

The effects of this prosperity were seen in the growing population of Bradford on Avon and in the area generally.

Daniel Defoe, more famous for his Gulliver's Travels, also wrote *A Tour through the Whole Island of Great Britain in 1724-26.* In this he said "They told me at Bradford on Avon that it is no extraordinary thing to have clothiers in that country worth from ten thousand to forty thousand a man and many of the great families who now pass for gentry in those counties have been originally raised from and built up by this truly noble manufacture.". John Hall's was one of them. He bought Great Chalfield for the sum of £5200 in 1673 when the area was reaching the height of this cloth based prosperity. It proved to be a wise acquisition with far reaching consequences. The probate value placed on it of £7000 after his death in 1710 shows it increased considerably in value during his ownership and that it was his second most valuable property after The Hall in Bradford on Avon.

One of the tangible results of his ownership was his generosity to All Saints Church Great Chalfield that has already been briefly mentioned. The beautiful silver paten, chalice and plate he presented have hallmarks dating them to 1680 and a motto *Deo et Ecclesiae,* for God and the Church, surmounted by a shield of arms with elaborate mantling, three axes for Hall and barry, (horizontal bars) of ten for Thynne, his wife's family, given shortly after he bought the manor. All three are still in use in this parish church for Holy Communion. So is the three decker pulpit he gave to All Saints with its three levels for the three orders of ministry: the laity, deacons and priests. He presented three Rectors to the parish Church as Patron between 1678 and 1707.

A great sadness for him and his two wives was that they had no children. This must have been behind the one scandal connected with him. It seems it did not come to light until after his death, but is apparent from his will made in 1708, proved in 1711 after his death. He took the precaution of having his wishes reinforced by Act of Parliament. Why all this caution? His sole heiress was a fifteen year old girl, Rachel Baynton of Little Chalfield., rather than his closest male heir. There is a very strong presumption that she was his illegitimate daughter. Trustees were appointed one of whose duties was to see she married with their approval. But even if they did not approve of her choice most unusually she was to receive a good deal of money. Her apparent father was Thomas Baynton of Little Chalfield, John Hall's nephew and a Thynne relative of John Hall's second wife. She had died childless in 1683 aged 32. Rachel's mother was Elizabeth nee Willoughby. Her true family name was not recorded until 1892! This was because an otherwise unattested daughter of John Hall's, Elizabeth, was later inserted into the family tree to regularise the situation. It looked better in the family tree! If Rachel was just a favourite neice, rather than a child of his old age, this subterfuge would not have been necessary. Rachel was born in Little Chalfield in 1695, twelve years after John Hall's second wife died .and was baptised in All Saints Great Chalfield

Her connection with the Manor she was to own began there. There is no mention in his will of sitting tenants of the kind that had rented it earlier. He had though introduced in 1679 farming tenants soon after he bought it – it was after all a business venture. It must not be forgotten that the house was placed in a manor of 500 acres. This is good farming land and could produce income for its tenants who also had use of the mill that was part of the manor.

Within six months of its purchase he had let it to William Wynne and Edward Wallis.and in 1679 to John Sertaine, still a local name. It was let again in 1685 to John Eyre of Little Chalfield so John Sertaine did not renew his lease. This is in the British Library and the detail with which it was drawn up is remarkable."Agreed with old John Sertain to let him Chalfield for £360 a year for seven years. I reserve the pigeon house and fishponds, timber trees and coppice wood and shroud (lopping) and timber field and hone (pig) field not to be ploughed nor any other ground that hath not lately been ploughed. I am to pay all taxes which shall be due by parliament (e.g. the chimney tax, 2 shillings a chimney) and he to hedge, ditch etc and keep bounds at his own charge." John Hall was a careful man. In fact leases of a farm for three lives were not unusual at that time.

The chalice given by John Hall to All Saints.

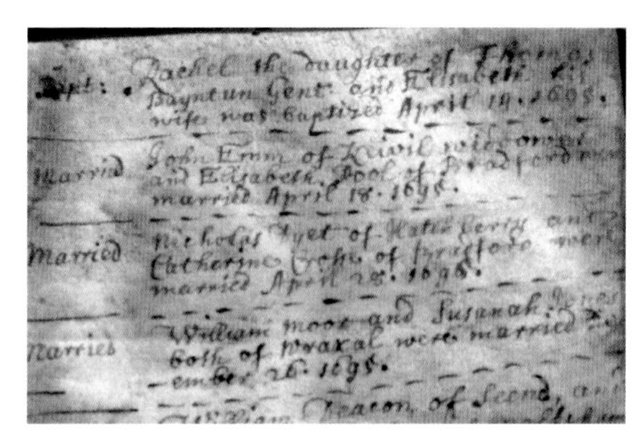
Bapt: Rachel the daughter of Thomas Baynton Gent: and Elizabeth his wife was baptized April 19 1695.

The entry in the register of All Saints of the baptism of Rachel Baynton in 1695

These created an incentive for the first two generations to improve the property and the income it generated, as happened with the families with the three long tenancies of Great Chalfield that came later.

Rachel Baynton was married a year after she inherited John Hall's fortune aged sixteen. This was no surprise. She married into the aristocracy like John Hall. Her husband was William Pierrepont heir to the Duke of Kingston upon Hull. Their extensive estates in Nottinghamshire were built on coal and they owned the docks in Hull from which to export it. Above all they were a very civilised and intelligent family. William's sister was Lady Mary Wortley Montagu, the most brilliant letter writer of her generation whose husband coincidentally was, as Sir John Eyre had been, Ambassador in Constantinople.

She travelled there with him and her letters while there to her friends are famous. She recorded that the local people inoculated their children with a weak form of smallpox to protect them from it. By a sad irony her brother died aged twenty one of that

Lady Mary Wortley Montagu
- the sister of William Pierrepont, Rachel's husband
(1689 - 1762)

disease soon after she returned. He had only been married two years. He and Rachel had two children. Lady Mary persuaded her father to have both grandchildren inoculated to avoid the fate of their father. This was successful. She also had success at court and persuaded the Royal family and many others at court to inoculate their children. She was painted in Turkish dress which became quite fashionable for a time.

Rachel was unlucky in her next relationship as the mistress of Lord Lumley, later to become Lord Scarborough. They had two children and he left her when she was pregnant with a third as soon as he inherited his title and estate from his father. Lady Mary Wortley Montagu wrote a poem about mistresses and included her in it. They did not get on and she was not let into the secret of Lady Mary's plans to elope. Lady Mary thought she might give them away. Rachel was left a proportion of her inheritance, including property in Bath which she administered herself. She also died young aged twenty seven in 1722. Her relations said it was of a broken heart when Lord Scarborough left her. Her son Evelyn inherited his title and estates from his grandfather when the first Duke died in 1726. He also inherited his father's land and property which included Great Chalfield. The Manor entered into a period of efficient administration by his agents. The deeds of all the 18th century tenancies survive in the 2nd Duke's papers, now in the British Library in London. They are simple business like documents with none of the detail of the one John Hall gave to John Sertaine. The first of these tenants were the Willis family, who were Quaker from Bromham.

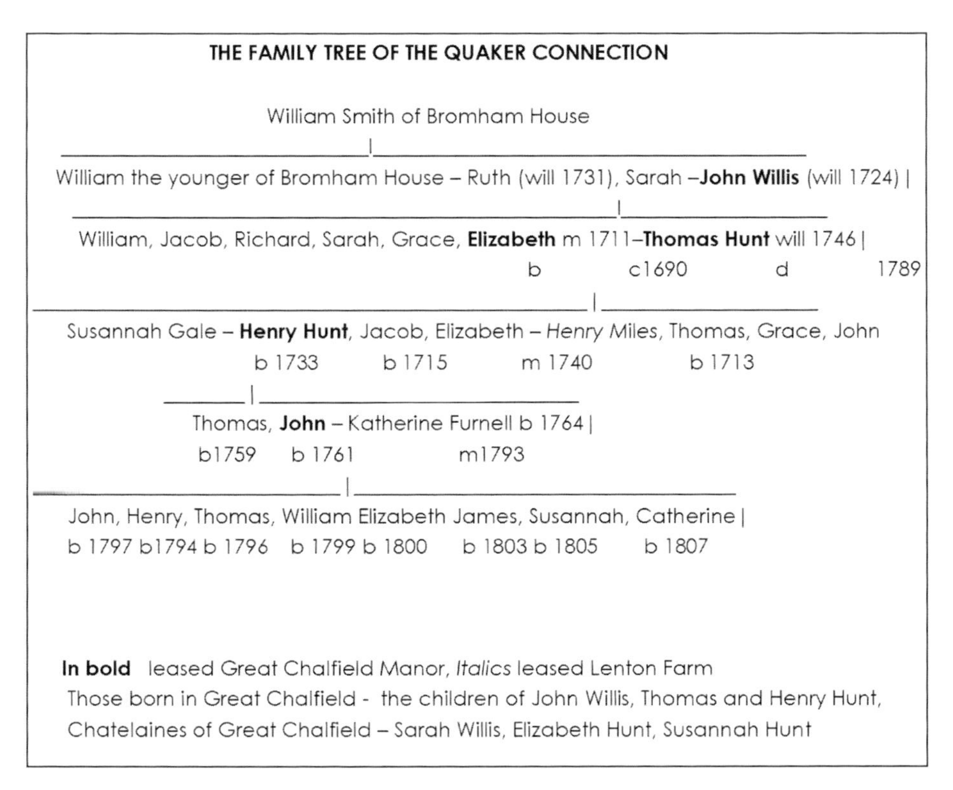

The family tree of the Hunts while they were tenants of Great Chalfield

Their daughter, Elizabeth, married Thomas Hunt and the tenancy passed to them in 1711. Thomas passed it to his widow, she passed it to their eldest son Henry. He passed it to his son John so it remained in the Hunt family for three generations. We learn much of them from these deeds and from their wills. Copies of these have recently been given to the Manor Library. They reveal that the Hunts too were Quakers. We know that a Quaker monthly meeting was held at Great Chalfield in February 1728, there were probably many more. Someone, probably a young Hunt, carved his initials on the stone round the oriel widow in the north bedroom in 1747, presumably just for fun or to record a marriage.

Wall plaque on the barn extention, with K for Kingston and the Hall family emblem, a homage to the Duke's mother

There is a plaque dated 1752 on the eighteenth century barn extension opposite the north wing of the manor which held stables etc.

The barn was extended in Henry Hunt's time. It has the three hatchets of John Hall's crest with a K for Kingston. This was a nice gesture of the Duke to his mother, Rachel, who inherited the manor from John Hall. The manor land was prospering, with increased yields from the recently introduced rotation of crops. Elizabeth Hunt died in Holt in 1789 aged one hundred. She lived in Great Chalfield before her marriage and then as a tenant at least until it was sold in 1769. Few have lived there so long. Members of the Hunt family still live in the area and contributed to recent woodland planting. They also loaned their fine child's galloping gig with two toy horses to Great Chalfield in 2014.

The Bigamous Duchess when young, English School.

The Second Duke, Evelyn Pierrepont, became famous after his death as a result of his widow's conviction for bigamy. He and Elizabeth Chudleigh had married late in life. When she became his mistress, many years before, she was a beautiful and socially brilliant woman. There were Chudleigh family estates in Devon but she was not well off. She had previously married Augustus John Hervey in 1744. This was kept secret so she would not lose her salary as Maid of Honour to the Princess of Wales. He was a naval captain and his elder brother was heir to the Earl of Bristol. What they neither of them could have known was his elder brother was to die childless and he became the second earl. Before all that they had drifted apart and she fell in love with the Duke of Kingston. After long years as his mistress, when she was forty eight they decided to marry. They consulted the Archbishop of Canterbury but she cannot have levelled completely because he gave them permission to go ahead. She had recently been ruled to be a spinster because no witness of her marriage to John Hervey could be found.

They were childless – a son of hers with John Hervey died in infancy. They had always lived extravagantly and the Duke built a huge house for them both in central London and called it Chudleigh House. It was renamed Kingston House when they married. The famous Casanova when he visited London was introduced to her and was hugely impressed. Thoresby Hall in Nottinghamshire had burned down in the early 1760s. The expense of rebuilding it and furnishing it to her exacting standards as well as their new house in London proved too great a strain even on the Duke's purse. He sold Great Chalfield in 1769 to help raise the necessary funds for all this building and the wedding. They were only married for four years. They went to Bath for his health in 1773. The receipts of the visit are to be found in the Egerton Papers in the British Library. He died soon afterwards. She had visited The Hall in Bradford on Avon but there is no record of their visiting Great Chalfield. He had so many properties he probably was only just aware of owning it. Anecdote has it he sold Monkton House nearby to his steward without knowing where it was. He was then shocked when he saw it while out hunting and his steward explained the story.

The Duke on his deathbed wrote Elizabeth's name into his will in a gap he had left especially for it. The family was horrified. They dug up the record of her first and only valid marriage to John Hervey and took her to court for bigamy. She was tried before the King's Bench in Westminster Hall. Huge numbers attended – it was a social event of the first magnitude as Robert Fuller's 1946 Guidebook to Great Chalfield had it. It took place in 1776 three years after the Duke's death in 1773 and was a ticket only occasion. A trial of a member of the aristocracy was a rare event and on such a charge was virtually unprecedented. Mrs Hannah Moore was there and described it for a friend."Garrick would have me take his ticket to go to the trial, a sight which for beauty and magnificence exceeded anything that those who were never present at a coronation or a trial by peers can imagine. Mr Garrick and I were in full dress by seven. When all were seated and the King at Arms had commanded silence on pain of imprisonment (which however was very ill observed) the Usher of the Black Rod was commanded to bring in his prisoner. She was dressed in deep mourning, a black hood on her head, her hair modestly dressed and powdered, a black silk saque with crape trimmings, black gauze, deep ruffles and black gloves. The Duchess has but small remains of that beauty of which Kings and princes were once so enamoured. She is large and ill shaped. There was nothing white but her face; and had it not been for that she would have looked like a bale of bombazeen". This was a heavy twill fabric, usually black and worn by widows so very suitable for such an occasion.

Elizabeth Hervey at her trial for bigamy in 1776
Isaac Taylor 1730 - 1807 © National Trust/Sue James

The trial lasted for five days with the family proving the bigamy but failing to get the money. The will was proved in her favour after nearly ten years of litigation. She became a countess from her first marriage but not a Duchess, though while she lived an amazingly colourful life on the continent after the trial she was always known as such. That and her jewels were her passport into the most exalted social circles wherever she went. She bought a chateau off the Duke of Orleans for £50000. She also bought three estates in Estonia with 7000 serfs and shipped there many trees and shrubs from Hull. She became a close friend of Catherine the Great and an established figure in the St Petersburg social scene. Sadly and perhaps inevitably she died alone in a flat in Paris in 1788 aged 68. When she died The Times declared of her very colourful life, "Bigamy it seems is a more notorious crime than simple fornication or fashionable adultery". An anonymous account of her life called "*An authentic detail of the particulars relative to the late Duchess of Kingston*" came out that same year. It has recently been reprinted and makes sad reading, despite the extraordinary life she had led. It includes a copy of her will translated from the French. She had been kind to her nephews and nieces. But she had spent an awful lot of their money.

Rachel Pierrepont's only daughter, Frances, had married and became Lady Frances Meadows. Her son Charles inherited the estate on the death of the 'Duchess'. This included all John Hall's property in Bath and the area. He became the Ist Earl Manvers. Some will be familiar with Manvers and Pierrepont Streets in Bath and Kingston Road in Bradford on Avon. All of the papers from the estate passed from the Manvers family to Nottingham University library. From there these were amalgamated with the Egerton Collection in the British Library in the second world war and can be consulted there, a very complete and rich set of documents covering this whole period in the history of Great Chalfield and its owners in the 17th and 18th centuries. This includes detailed estate accounts from 1726-1780 and many documents from the Hall family before then. Great Chalfield was separated from the estate and sold by the Duke before the Manvers' time to Robert Neale MP c1706-1776, a wealthy cloth merchant of Shaw House nr Melksham, whose business was centred on Corsham.

Chapter 3 1769-1878

When Robert Neale bought Great Chalfield for £15000 in 1769 he cannot have been aware of the tragedies that were to hit his family in the next ten years. All seemed well at first. He had a son, also Robert, who married a wealthy London wine merchant's daughter, Grace Goldstone, in 1770, the year after his father bought the manor. They had a daughter, also called Grace, in the following year. Another daughter Lydia followed in 1773. Then disaster struck with the death of the girls' father in the same year Lydia was born. Robert senior made a new will in 1774 leaving Great Chalfield to his eldest granddaughter Grace and his nephew John Neale of Berkeley. This was to ensure it did not go to his son's wife. Evidently he disliked her. The daughters had been baptised in St Clement Dane's, Westminster and perhaps he felt they could become too much under their mother's family's control Their father was buried in All Saints Great Chalfield to which Robert added a new chapel in 1775 of Gothic Revival design, now the Vestry. As head of the family Robert also set about building a family vault under the chancel in 1775. Sadly he was to be its first occupant when he died in 1776. His son's remains were also placed there and his wife's transferred to it from Corsham. Grace had lost first her father and then her grandfather in the space of three years.

She lived in London with her mother's family, the Goldstones and the estates she had inherited which were considerable were administered by trustees until she married. They largely neglected Great Chalfield manor, though there was some activity. 80 acres of woodland from it were clear felled and not replanted in the next 20 years. Demand for wheat was rising. A vivid picture of what the place was like then can be found in a footnote in the architect John Chessell Buckler's study of The Royal Palace at Eltham published in 1828: he wrote of Great Chalfield, soon to be ranked among the finest surviving domestic buildings of its time, "Neglect and decay are visible in every part of the edifice and comfort and convenience are disregarded, provided the rooms shelter the grain and the roads which convey it thither enable loaded wagons to pursue their sluggish course." Very vivid. Things were no better in 1834 when in an article in The Gentleman's Magazine the author wrote "The hand of time is permitted to proceed without a helper in its gradual work of dilapidation." The Trustees did not give its maintenance a very high priority and the Spackmans kept things going there as best they could by farming and milling.

Grace had had a very privileged upbringing. Aged 16 she was introduced to Pitt the Younger in the deanery of St Paul's after a service of thanksgiving for the recovery of George III in 1787. She later claimed this gave her a lifelong interest in politics. She also, after a sad start to her life, had a happy marriage though she and her husband remained childless. Her husband was Sir Harry Burrard (1765-1840)
Already a very distinguished naval officer, he added Neale to his name when he married Grace in 1795 in London when she was twenty four and he was six years older. He was captain of the Royal Yacht for a while and for many years Groom of the Bedchamber of George III. He saw much active service during his naval career. He got a special vote of thanks from Parliament after his ship did not join in the mutiny at the Nore.

He rose to the rank of Admiral in 1810 and was made Commander of the Mediterranean fleet in 1825. He and his wife lived in Walhampton House near Lymington where he was MP for twenty seven years. They entertained the King and Queen in 1801 and 1804 at their home while the Royal Family was holidaying at Weymouth. One of the reasons for this friendship was that Grace was Lady in Waiting to the Queen and the constant companion of Princess Amelia who would have been with them for their visits.

Sir Harry Burrard Neale as a young naval officer.

King George III with his Queen and six daughters
William Rought. The Royal Collection

Letters between them survive which show their great affection for one another. He was clearly a great man. When he died in 1840 an obelisk was erected by public subscription outside Lymington to commemorate him. The inscription at its base outlines his very distinguished career and of his virtues it singles out 'the beauty of his humility'.

From the point of view of the history of Great Chalfield Grace and her husband's interest in it was crucial. This was shown clearly in 1822 when they bought out her Neale relatives' half share in it for £7904. The Rector of All Saints Great Chalfield Richard Warner FSA (1763-1857), whom they appointed in 1809, also clearly loved it and had a vital part to play in its history. His wife's mother was buried there in 1832 aged 89 though by then they lived in Castle Cary. He was an interesting man with strong antiquarian interests. He became a prolific author and was well connected in architectural circles as a result. As he had been brought up for a while in the Burrard Neale's home in Hampshire as a boy Grace and Harry knew him very well. He doubtless pointed out to them the growing architectural importance of Great Chalfield.

Interest in medieval architecture was growing. This interest and the fashion for building in the medieval style had started in a small way with follies in the grounds of great houses at the end of the 18th century. The Gothic Revival gathered momentum as more and more people came to admire the gothic style with its pointed arches rather than neo-classical buildings like St Pauls in London and many others built in the previous two hundred years. These imitated the Greek and Roman remains that were much admired on the Grand Tour. Gothic Revival was also fuelled in 1829 by Catholic Emancipation, after which Roman Catholics could build churches of their own for the first time since the Reformation – and they favoured the medieval architecture of the churches taken from them at that time. Examples of medieval churches were easy to find. Examples of good domestic medieval architecture, unmodified and unchanged, were much thinner on the ground.

Architects, especially in London, needed to satisfy their clients' wishes when they were asked to design houses in this style. Come the hour, come the man. Augustus Pugin and later his son of the same name had the passion and skill to record these buildings and publish their studies. John Britton was also important with his publication in five volumes which came out from 1807- 1826 of Architectural Antiquities of Great Britain.

He described his studies of buildings using a new architectural vocabulary which caught on. They tended to be idealised. Those of the Pugins were really accurate and so more useful to copy. Britton's papers were placed in the Devizes museum when he died – he was a Wiltshire man.
John Buckler was another architect and artist of that period. He and his son John Chessell Buckler visited the house twice and left behind six watercolours of it commissioned by the owners.

John Buckler wrote to his friend John Gage in October 1823 after these visits and said about the manor "Great Chalfield, I am bold to declare, is one of the noblest remains of domestic architecture in England". High praise indeed. This interest in the manor led to an article in the Gentleman's Magazine about it in 1834. This in turn led Sir Harry Burrard to invite a pupil of Augustus Pugin the elder (1769-1832), Thomas Larkins Walker, to come to the house in 1836 and record it. His detailed study, made with two architect colleagues, was published in 1837 in Part II of the series *Examples of Gothic Architecture* that had been begun by Pugin, his mentor.

The Great Hall, Great Chalfield
Watercolour John Chessel Buckler 1823

A Plate illustrating the Screen in the Great Hall
Thomas Larkins Walker Examples of Gothic Architecture 1837

In the preface to this publication he described Great Chalfield as “one of the archetypal houses of late medieval England.” The younger Augustus Pugin (1812-52) had subscribed for three copies of this when subscriptions were invited in 1836 before its publication. He was then living near Salisbury and was obviously already well aware that his father’s pupil’s study of the house would be of use to him in his own work.

His interest takes on added significance because all these architects at that time became excited by the competition to appoint someone to rebuild the Palace of Westminster, destroyed by fire in 1834. The terms of this competition were announced in 1835 and the result announced in 1836, Charles Barry and Augustus Pugin first JC Buckler second!

The prize winning entry in the competition won by Barry and Pugin 1836 37

For the next few years Barry and Pugin were working on their detailed plans, without doubt helped by ideas Pugin had found in Thomas Larkins Walker’s invaluable study of

Great Chalfield. Their first collaboration had been to design and build a new school for the Governors of King Edward's Birmingham.
They worked on this together just before their collaboration on the Palace of Westminster. The school building in Birmingham has been demolished, though plans and photographs of it remain. In this building there are strong reminders of the Great Hall of Great Chalfield and especially its screen. The Palace of Westminster still stands as a record of their work together and also contains echoes of Great Chalfield.
This combination of circumstances made Sir Harry Burrard's Commission for a study of the manor important because of its timing and its place in the Gothic Revival.

The schoolroom of King Edward's Birmingham designed by Barry and Pugin 1837 - 38

Great Chalfield Manor from the garden c1860

It also was supremely important in view of the state of the house then. Inevitably something had to happen as a result of the process of decay at Great Chalfield that had been noted earlier in the century. This was getting progressively worse as decay of this kind always does if nothing is done about it. William Spackman and his wife were members of a trusted Corsham family. They were farming tenants and millers from 1825-c1875. Their tenancy began just two years after Sir Harry and Grace had become sole owners of Great Chalfield by buying out her cousin John Neale's half share in the manor. This was a very considerable investment. The Spackmans repaid this trust in their long stay. William Spackman's wife succeeded him in due course as a tenant after his death. They became more and more uncomfortable living there and became worried about the state of parts of the roof. They eventually got permission from Sir Harry in 1838 to divide the Great Hall horizontally to make a compact farm house of it, with windows on its ground floor. At the same time or soon after much of the East wing was demolished and new mullioned windows were created looking out to the gardens.

This involved taking the roof off this part of the house as it had become unsafe and removing the solar fire place to lessen the load on the floor. Bosses on the ceiling of the great hall were damaged by putting up an artificial ceiling for the bedrooms on the first floor and at some point the screen was removed. Photographs taken later show what a complete job they made of all this. Fortunately Thomas Larkins Walker's drawings of all of it had been published a few years before.

Nina Hobhouse, Robert Fuller's only sister, drew Great Chalfield in 1888. Later she made a lovely free water colour of her brother's new Summerhouse (see page 74).

It remains a mystery why Sir Harry did not go ahead with the restoration that had been promised to Thomas Larkins Walker in 1836. But all the essential qualities of the house remained and were enough to inspire later owners to take up this challenge. Sir Harry died in 1840, just two years after allowing this demolition. In his will, which is in the large collection of Great Chalfield papers in the Wiltshire and Swindon History Centre, perhaps surprisingly he made little provision for Grace. The reason he stated was that she had private means from her family. As a widow she went to live in London. Walhampton House, their married home in the New Forest which is now a prep school, went to Sir Harry's brother, the Revd George Burrard who unlike Grace and Harry had children who would enjoy it as a family home. Great Chalfield, which Grace had brought to the marriage, also passed to Sir Harry's brother. He died a year later and it then passed to his widow, Emma Lady Burrard.

An interesting insight into the life of the manor at this time is provided by the Visitors Book, preserved in the Library. It was presented in 1857 to Mrs William Spackman and her family by the Wiltshire Archaeological and History Society in remembrance of the welcome given to them on their visit on 12th August of that year.

The society had been founded four years before and still flourishes. We may assume they were welcomed into the Great Hall, by then subdivided into the separate quarters where the Spackmans lived. In the first years recorded in the book there were an average of 50 visitors a year. Some from far afield. Its fame had spread. Mr CH Talbot of Lacock Abbey visited in 1860.

The East Wing in 1907, its roof had been removed in 1838 for safety.

One of the most significant visits in the whole history of the Manor took place that same year. This was by George Fuller, its future owner who laid the foundations of its modern history. Other members of the family had visited in 1857. The Fuller family lived in Neston Park just up the road to the north. George's grandfather John had bought it in 1801 when he moved there from Leatherhead. They were a family of substantial wealth, descended through their Fleetwood relatives from Oliver Cromwell's youngest daughter Bridget. George was the second son who was to inherit when his father died ten years after this visit in 1860. He inherited because his elder brother had been tragically killed in the Crimean War. Fullers still live at Neston Park, successor to a house that Thomas Tropenell lived in before he built Great Chalfield.

The significance of George's visit is that he was impressed enough to buy it in December 1878, eighteen years later, when it came on the market. This purchase ranks in the long history of the House alongside that of Thomas Hanham. It began a new era as Thomas Hanham's had done and both rescued the house when it was in a state of decay. Without the continuing interest of George Fuller's family and their direct descendants, the Floyds, together with its repair and maintenance by the National Trust since the Manor was presented to it by Robert Fuller in 1943, it would undoubtedly by now be an elegant ruin, if it was here at all.

Chapter Four 1878 -2019

Emma Lady Burrard's sale of Great Chalfield in 1878 was of interest legally because it was the first time in its long history that it had been sold by a woman. Because of the Married Woman's Property Act of 1870 she owned it in her own right. Anne Eyre in 1553, Rachel Baynton in 1711 and Grace Burrard in 1776 had all inherited it but had to hand it over to their husbands. Lady Burrard put it on the market for £25000. When George Fuller of Neston Park bought it he reunited the estates of Neston Park and Great Chalfield for the first time since they were both owned by Thomas Tropenell, the builder of Great Chalfield. He would have been pleased. By then parts of it were in a sorry state. The Great Hall, converted since 1838 into a two storied 'farmhouse', was still occupied by tenants who farmed the land but the rest of the house was slowly decaying. On purchasing the manor George Fuller had agreed terms with tenants, James and Anna Bailey, who had a son James and two resident servants, Frances Dash and Maud Church.

The Baileys became equally devoted to it and encouraged George Fuller not to demolish it but to improve the land drains instead. They moved out in 1904 into another house provided for them. George's fourth son Robert loved the place and had the fishing rights in the streams,leat and moats from his father for one shilling a year from 1903. By 1905 he was in a position to offer to restore it because of his success with the Avon Rubber Company in Melksham. His father had bought an interest in this firm in 1897 when it was in need of capital from a strong sense of public duty. He was the Liberal MP for Westbury from 1885-1895 and held strong reforming views.

He had earlier bought a share in an ailing brewery in Chiswick when he was offered a partnership in it. This prospered. On this success was built the Fuller, Smith and Turner business which recently agreed to sell the worldwide product marketing of Fuller's London Pride Ales to Asahi Co of Japan.

The Entrance Hall with staircase to the upper floor with the Bailey's furnishings.1880 - 1903

A bedroom in the upper floor of the Great Hall 1880 - 1903

Fullers coined the slogan '*Beers of honest repute*', which sounds just right and as early as 1889 put it on promotional hot air balloons in the skies above London.

His son Robert had trained in electrical engineering at Faraday House in London and won the Gold Medal there in 1896.
His prize books are in the house library. He joined the Avon Tyre Company at his father's suggestion and rose rapidly to managing director in 1898. He installed electric power in the factory and was well placed to take advantage of the growing demand for car and cycle tyres.

George Fuller MP of Neston Park who purchased the manor in 1878

By 1906 sales exceeded £100000 a year and they were turning out 1000 cycle tyres a month.In 1903 his father had asked the Corsham architect Harold Brakspear to provide a report with costings for restoring Great Chalfield. The report is in five sections and the estimate came to £3850. By 1905 his son Robert felt sufficiently confident of his success in business to lease the house from his father and take over this project. Recent research has shown the very detailed interest he took in every aspect of this right through to the completion of the project in 1913. Perhaps needless to say the costs rose sharply. Restoration of the east wing proved more complicated than was first envisaged.

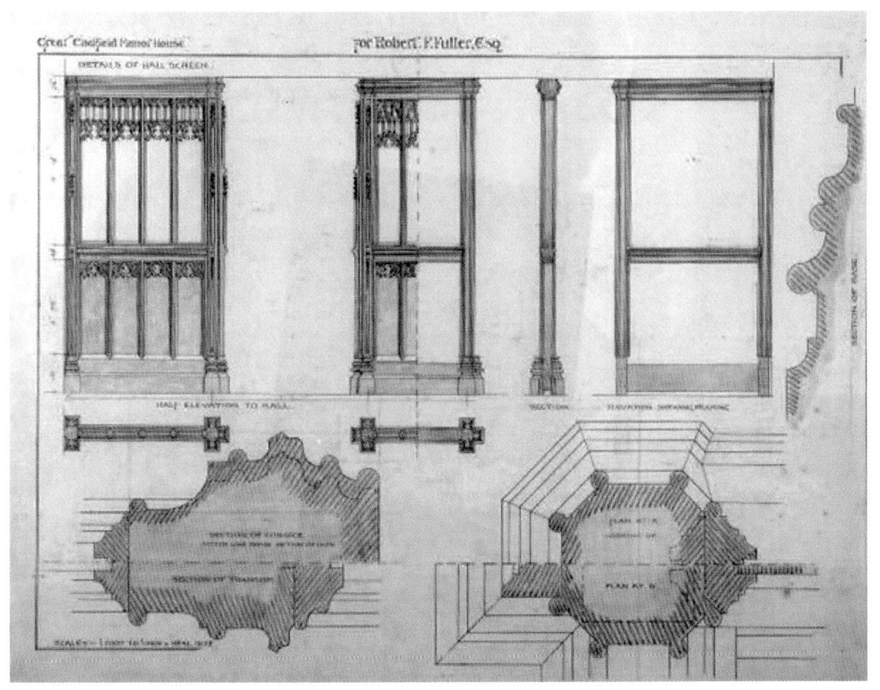

Sir Harold Brakspear's drawing, copied from T L Walker to create a replica oak screen made by Downing and Rudman for Robert Fuller.

The eventual solution has kept the character and outline of it as far as was possible but the rooms in it became more in keeping with the residence of an Edwardian gentleman, with its library and private sitting room. Builder's costs for 1909 alone for example were £2588, the year the replica screen in the Great Hall was put in place. There was also the cost of adding a minstrels' gallery above the screen. There had not been one before but this addition to make the hall more suited for entertainment was entirely in character with the period of the house. Others of the same date have one.
Robert Fuller always responded quickly to the architect's letters. They frequently disagreed. Feelings sometimes ran high but always a mutually satisfactory solution was found. No one, lay or expert, has ever found fault with the sympathy for the house they both showed. It has been hailed as the most successful restoration of the National Trust properties of that period. It is not surprising that Harold Brakspear was invited to restore St George's Chapel Windsor later, for which he was knighted. His success in the restoration of Great Chalfield was in part down to the detailed plans of the house and drawings of all its architectural features by Thomas Larkins Walker and to the water colours of the Bucklers father and son made in 1823 at Sir Harry Burrard Neale's request. These were done before any of the 19th century changes took place.

Photographs taken before and after Brakspear's work show the skills of both owners and architect in this highly productive project. Walker's records for example enabled them to identify fragments of the original stone work found in the garden which were incorporated and gave further valuable clues as to size and style. The restoration of the fireplace in the solar was particularly ingenious. They used fragments of it rescued from

the garden to recreate the Elizabethan fireplace installed by Anne and John Eyre to replace a smaller one put there when the house was built. This was the only thing not drawn by Thomas Larkins Walker. He declared it to be ‘in meretricious bad taste” to use his own words. It was Elizabethan not medieval.
In all it was an eminently practical restoration. It included a new engine house for the waterworks, heated motor houses with their own repair pit, a forge, new stables, a woodshed and a potting shed. Robert surely had a big hand in all that. The old stables and malt house above running north from the west side of the house became an extension of the private quarters with a servant’s hall on the north end, a successful early Edwardian 'barn conversion'. The 17th century dove house at the end of it became servants' rooms with maids above and footmen below, separated by a laundry and luggage lift. This whole wing needed chimneys and windows which were the subject of lengthy correspondence. Robert Fuller won the day as he generally did. The debate was over the chimneys mainly, which now look as if they have always been there. They are so right for the house. Robert and especially his future wife, Mabel, were very interested in All Saints Church and commissioned the architect CH Biddulph Pinchard to restore it. This restoration took place between 1912 and 1922 and was very sensitive.

One of the most inspired things Robert Fuller did was to commission Alfred Parsons RA, PRWS to design a garden round the house. This area from the mid nineteenth century had been made into a vegetable garden by the farming tenants on the old lawn or pleasance. It is now one of the most beautiful Arts and Crafts gardens in the country. This is thanks to Alfred

Parson's brilliant designs and structures and to the present chatelaine, Patsy Floyd's, inspired recreation of them. Alfred Parsons had become one of the most eminent garden designers of his day. He built his own lovely house and garden in Broadway in 1911. This was in the centre of a glittering circle of his American friends. He was also a leading watercolourist and President of the Royal Watercolour Society. His framework and choice of trees for the garden were particularly sensitive.

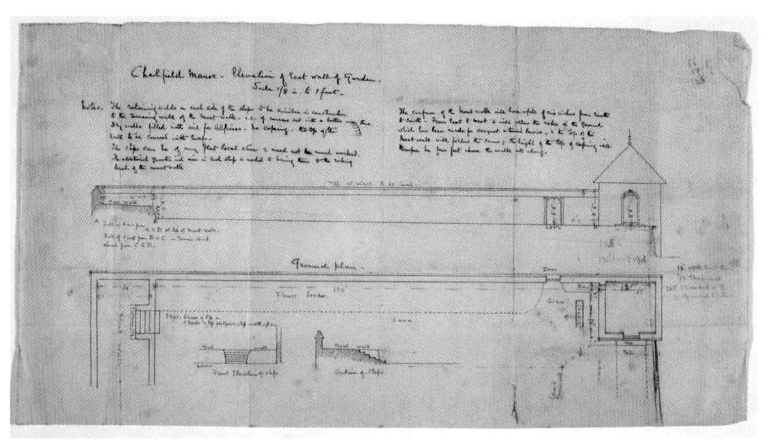

Alfred Parsons' design for a Summer House similar to Gravetye Manor

He made extensive changes. The terrace was created and the beautiful summer house and cheese store at the end of it was built near the Norman mill that was in use until 1878. It then became part of the mill cottages for the garden and household staff. The summer house is very similar to that created by Ernest George for Alfred Parson's friend William Robinson, the garden writer, at Gravetye Manor in Sussex Here also Harold Brakspear created detailed plans to fit Parson's designs. The wall round the church yard was extended to mark the present boundaries of the garden. The terrace was created with roll top coping on the boundary wall. He kept the medieval fish

ponds that were fed from the spring that also then provided Broughton Gifford and Holt with fresh piped drinking water. He filled in the stew ponds in the orchard just above them but kept the fine ancient orchard.
The drainage of the site was addressed in a bold way at the same time. The level of the ground to the north and the south of the house and under the Great Hall was lowered by two feet. The line of trees to the north of the house was planted to create a vista and the flagstones from the Great Hall were made into a patio to the south of the house. This filled the area to the south and east of the present house that had been surrounded by service wings that were taken down in the 17th century. Ventilation bricks were added to the base of the north and south walls and a new sprung oak floor put into the Great hall for dancing, with central heating pipes along the south and east walls.

Robert Fuller had become engaged during this project to Mabel Chappell (1878-1968), an heiress of the Chappell music publishing family in London. She was the ideal partner both for him and for his great restoration project. She was interested in the Arts and Crafts movement and her books on this subject, some from her unmarried days, are still in the library. They were married in the Parish Church in Corsham in 1911. This appropriately was where Thomas Tropenell and his wife and children were buried in a handsome family tomb.

The Garden House 1912 by Georgina Hobhouse
C/o the History Centre, Chippenham WSA3581

The bunting for George V's coronation was up in the town which made the approach to the Church a very festive sight. She was thirty three when they married. She wore a Lucille dress for the wedding. Lucille (Lucy, Lady Duff Gordon) was the leading dress designer of her day. This rare creation is now in The Bath Costume Museum. It is virtually the only example of Lucille's work in this country, the rest are all in America. This was a very grand wedding indeed. The bride was well up to the task of moving into the newly restored house.

This was a considerable challenge. There was no furniture left in it after the Baileys moved out. The collection the Fullers made is still in place and shows their expertise and good taste. Their catalogues and scholarly books on medieval furniture in the library show how carefully they went about it. Mabel was like her husband dedicated to public service of many kinds. She became a Commandant in the Red Cross for which she received an OBE. The whole was completed in 1916 by a new architect, CH Biddulph-Pinchard. He placed a second, half timbered, storey on the south west extension as a nursery after Robert and Mabel had a daughter, Mary.

She and Robert took the decision after a family conference to give the Manor House, with a trust fund, furniture, cartulary and Mill cottages to the National Trust in 1943, with land-scape covenants over the adjoining land. They continued to live on in the house until Robert died in 1955. Mabel retired to Broughton Gifford where she died in 1968. Mary (1916-1996) inherited the farm from her father.

Mabel and Robert Fuller c 1935

She married first in 1938 John Boyle of the Royal Scots Fusiliers who was killed near Anzio (1944) and secondly Charles Floyd in 1948. Charles Floyd came from a military family and as a pioneer of nature conservation founded the Wiltshire Wildlife Trust. Mary spent most of her long and fruitful life in Great Chalfield. She gave her tapestries to the National Trust and was devoted to Great Chalfield as her parents had been. She spent her last few years in Broughton Gifford.

The beautiful window in the side chapel is dedicated to her, her husbands and parents. The Parable of the Sower was her favourite among the Parables, it provides an opportunity to celebrate the wildlife on her beautiful farm here. Her fourth son Robert with his wife, Pats Vigors, moved into the house with their sons in 1985.

Robert was High Sheriff 2009-10 and undertakes a wide variety of public service in the county. Patsy has replanted the garden following the spirit of Alfred Parson's design.

Robert and Patricia Floyd

Parson's plans are in the Wiltshire and Swindon History Centre and have been the subject of modern study. Patsy has photographed the house and garden extensively over the last twenty five years and has made the garden the wonderful and widely admired place it is today. She has had the constant help of Neil Brocklehurst, their gardener, who came to Great Chalfield in 1987. Neil and his family live in the Mill Cottages.

The Floyds have together overseen the extensive programmes in the house and grounds undertaken by the National Trust with the assistance of The Manpower Service Commission crews and their successors and now especially with the support of a team of volunteers who help in the garden and another team who guide visitors round the house. Robert purchased adjoining land that overlooked the house in 1990 and the National Trust purchased 280 acres from him in 1994 for the permanent protection of the manor. He has recently planted two new woodlands and created wildlife corridors to conserve the rich flora and fauna. The five farm woodlands now amount to 10% of the whole area of 350 acres, of which 200 are in arable and the balance in permanent grass, which he farms with low inputs.

Great Chalfield remains a family home. But at the same time it is being put to an ever growing number of uses. This means that it is now better known and more widely loved than it has ever been in its long history. Visitors to it often remark on its beauty and tranquillity but it is also being chosen as a dramatic setting by an increasing number of film and television companies. They see it as a place where time seems to have stood still and their stories of the past easily come alive. But its sense of timeless tranquility, while real, is also deceptive. This brief account of its first 550 years shows that in fact its history has been remarkably eventful. As a result the lives of those who have lived in it have their own interest and also deserve to be told.

Acknowledgements
I have been greatly helped in my researches and the drafting of this story of the manor by a number of people. Special thanks are due to Pam Slocombe for sharing her knowledge of the sources, to Ivor Slocombe for numerous transcriptions from them, to Dr Linda Clark of History of Parliament for keeping me informed of the latest entries on all those MPs connected with the Manor and for her helpful comments and corrections of earlier drafts, to Timothy Brittain-Caitlin of the Department of Architecture at Kent University for help and advice on the Manor's role in the Gothic revival and to Mike Garwood for sharing his recent research into the life of Anne Carew, the wife of Christopher Tropenell. I am also most grateful to Robert Floyd for his advice and encouragement and finally to the Friends of Great Chalfield for their support.

Recommended further reading

History of Parliament The Commons 1422-1461 (VolVII 2019) sv Thomas Tropenell, 1386-1421 sv Sir Walter Hungerford, 1509-58 sv John Eyre, 1558-1603 sv Sir William Eyre, 1604-29 sv Sir John Eyre.
Oxford Dictionary of National Biography for members of the Hungerford family, in particular Robert Lord Moleyns and Sir Thomas Hungerford of Rowden.
Warp and Weft The Somerset and Wiltshire Woollen Industry Kenneth Rogers, Barracuda Books Ltd 1986
The Wool trade in Tudor and Stuart England PJ Bowden Frank Cass 1971
Pashas Traders and Travellers in the Islamic World James Mather, Yale University Press 2009

This Orient Isle Elizabethan England and the Islamic World Jeremy Brotton, Allen Lane 2016
An Authentic detail of the Particulars Relative to the Late Duchess of Kingston 1788 Nabu Public Domain Reprints
Lady Mary Wortley Montagu Isobel Grundy OUP 1999
The Wild Gardener, William Robinson, Francis Lincoln Ltd 2008, ISBN 13/978/0/7112/2542.

For the primary sources:
The British Library Thoresby Hall Collection, *Egerton Manuscripts* cat 2533 ff and 3650-60
Nottingham University Library: www Catalogue *sv The Manvers Collection*
The Wiltshire and Swindon History Centre in Chippenham for many documents from the manorial archive of Great Chalfield.

Thomas Tropenell Builder of Great Chalfield 2005 Hugh Wright available at the house
Great Chalfield Manor, The Builder and the Building 2019 Hugh Wright available as an offprint at the house.

Wiltshire & Swindon History Centre - www.wshc.eu

There is an extensive study collection of material relating to the history of the Manor, the Manor House and the county of Wiltshire in the House library, including the first Visitors' Book, the 1946 Guide Book written by Robert Fuller and recent studies of the history of the house and garden. This is accessible for research by prior written arrangement.

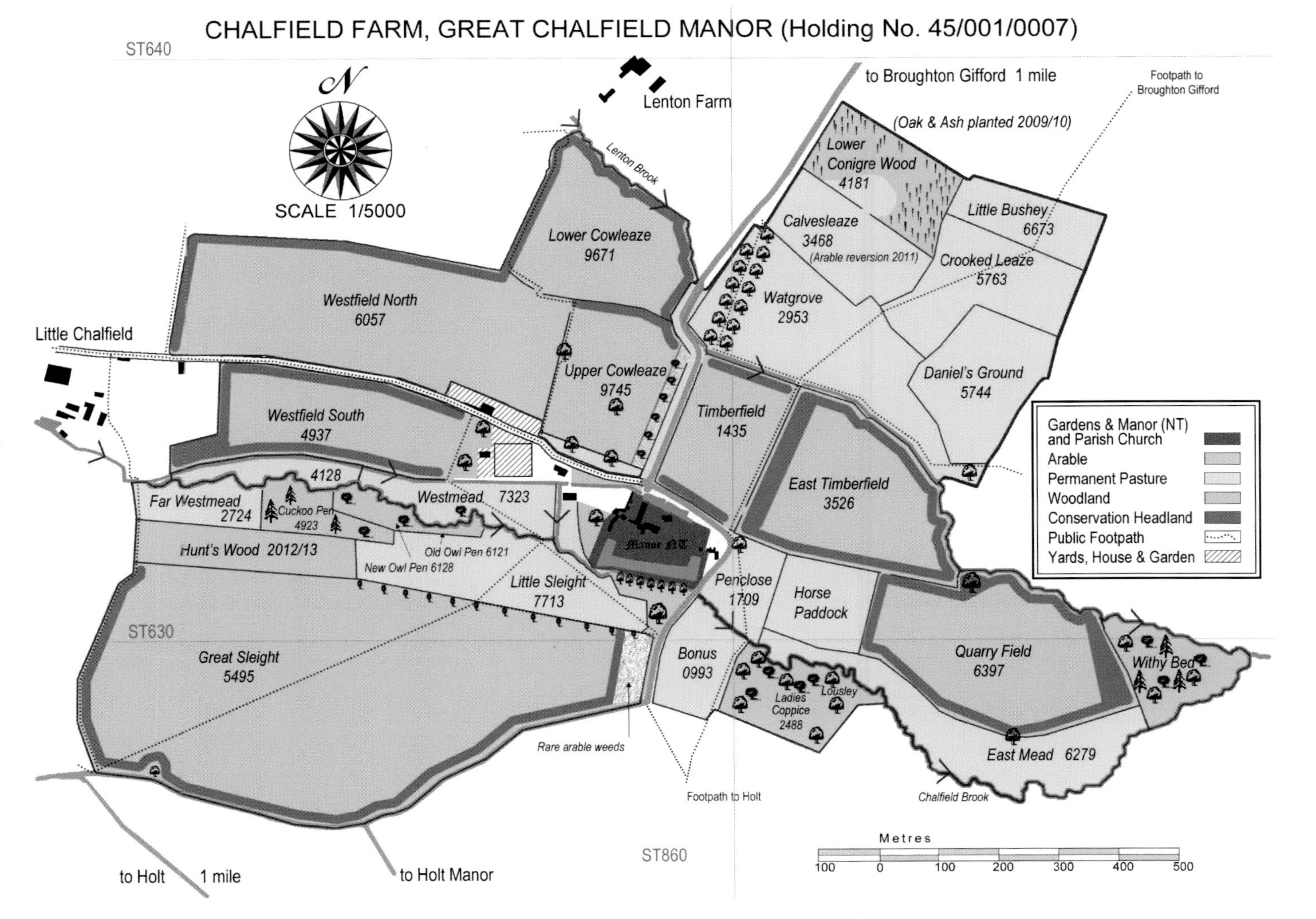

CHALFIELD FARM, GREAT CHALFIELD MANOR (Holding No. 45/001/0007)
ST640
SCALE 1/5000
Lenton Farm
to Broughton Gifford 1 mile
Footpath to Broughton Gifford
(Oak & Ash planted 2009/10)
Lenton Brook
Lower Conigre Wood 4181
Little Bushey 6673
Calvesleaze 3468
(Arable reversion 2011)
Crooked Leaze 5763
Lower Cowleaze 9671
Westfield North 6057
Watgrove 2953
Little Chalfield
Upper Cowleaze 9745
Daniel's Ground 5744
Timberfield 1435
Westfield South 4937
Gardens & Manor (NT) and Parish Church
Arable
Permanent Pasture
Woodland
Conservation Headland
Public Footpath
Yards, House & Garden
4128
East Timberfield 3526
Far Westmead 2724
Cuckoo Pen 4923
Westmead 7323
Hunt's Wood 2012/13
Old Owl Pen 6121
New Owl Pen 6128
Manor NT
Little Sleight 7713
Penclose 1709
Horse Paddock
ST630
Great Sleight 5495
Bonus 0993
Quarry Field 6397
Withy Bed
Ladies Coppice 2488
Lousley
Rare arable weeds
East Mead 6279
Footpath to Holt
Chalfield Brook
Metres
100
0
100
200
300
400
500
ST860
to Holt 1 mile
to Holt Manor